# Jack Fieldhouse
# Early Years

Early Years
© Jack Fieldhouse

ISBN 978-1-908904-49-2

Published by Northern Bee Books, 2013
Scout Bottom Farm
Mytholmroyd
Hebden Bridge
HX7 5JS (UK)

Design and artwork
D&P Design and Print
Worcestershire

Printed by Lightning Source, UK

# Jack Fieldhouse
# Early Years

Northern Bee Books

# Introduction

Jack Fieldhouse, known to me as "Uncle Jack", although he is my first cousin once removed, is a remarkable man who has lived a remarkable and very long life. His autobiography describes not only his wartime experiences, but also his love of art and of Nature. Jack's philosophy, of trying to live a life that works with, rather than against, the grain of Nature, is especially important given the seemingly exorable rise in global population and consumption that is damaging the planet for future generations. Jack doesn't just talk the talk: he lives a life that reflects his beliefs and values. In this there is an important lesson for us all.

*Lord Krebs*
*Jesus College*
*Oxford*
*August 2013*

A TRICKETT GIRL Showing
off her florel underwear!

# Jack Fieldhouse - A Yorkshire Lad Early Years

I, Jack Fieldhouse, was born in Attercliffe, December 1919. *J had one brother Bob born in…and no* sisters). Father, Ambrose, was a steel chemist at British Steel Sheffield. He became their chief Metallurgical Chemist and he married Florence Fieldhouse, an Artist, at Durdle Door in Dorset. They conveniently had the same name!

My father owned properties in Clifford Street, Brightside, Sheffield and they moved into one of them. It was a street like any other street in the Rother Valley, soot and sulphuric vapours pouring out of the steelworks of Rotherham and Sheffield blackened the houses.

One clear memory of our living there was that Dad bought a settee of strong material stuffed with straw. Both my brother and I bounced on the headrest, which assumed the shape of a camel's back.

Everywhere there were carthorses pulling drays for moving pig iron, steel bars or finished shapes for all manner of intentions - naval, engineering or armaments.

From Clifford Street we moved to a slightly up-market house in Sherwood Crescent off Wellgate, but still in Rotherham. The new house had a small garden bordered by a high, stone wall. A space between each house allowed access to the rear.

There were of course other families that seemed to have a plethora of girls. There was one Trickett boy with four sisters all about our age. The Trickett girls being slightly older would escort us to the local sweetie shop in Wellgate. We had our Saturday pennies and the counter was high so we tiptoed to slide our coin onto the counter proper. I remember the smiling face of the shopkeeper peering down at me, her hair cascading like a shower of candyfloss. And sometimes she gave a halfpenny change to my delight

Sweet sucking was the order of the day. We sucked our way home hand in hand with a Trickett girl. At the age of seven or eight I made an important decision, as I was involved in whispered talk about little boys and little girls. As Connie Atkinson was my best friend, I turned to her for an answer to my question, and simply asked if I could see her tummy.

At that time I didn't consider it cheeky, rude or indecent. I just wanted to see - a simple bout of curiosity! Come the moment and the elasticated curtain that concealed the view was drawn back and the view exposed. It was clean, pinky white in colour and with creases. The elastic was released rather hurriedly and snapped back into normal position, a bit like a catapult. Did Connie wince? I said "Sorry Connie" and the moment of discovery was over, my first and last anatomy lesson concluded and I thought at the time that I wouldn't want to do it a second time.

There is only one memory that comes easily! Dad made a little shed for my big black guinea pig and to my horror one afternoon I went into the garden to see a large black cat on the hutch. It shot out, holding the guinea pig in its mouth ran across the garden, up the wall and made its escape along the top of the wall. What anguish! There was nothing anyone could do, the guinea pig was bound to have been consumed and the cat would no doubt spend hours digesting it on some fire hearth.

My friend Connie Atkinson with flowers

# St Bedes

Bob and I attended the primary school of St Bede's, Masborough, three quarters of a mile away, and often Aunt Agnes who lived in St Anne's Road, a half mile in a different direction, escorted us there. Under the arches of an extension bridge was housed a number of horses, all large cart horses and we spent minutes leaning over the dirty wall to watch the comings and goings of the draymen. The roads were made of wood blocks and set in tar and on hot summer days the black liquid oozed up to the surface. It was eagerly collected by Fieldhouse fingers, made into a ball and presented to Mother on getting home. We thought she would be pleased but the reverse was the truth and having to find somewhere in the yard she had to start the business of cleaning two pairs of disgusting hands.

The Catholic church of St. Bede was huge, with large windows blackened by soot, which allowed little light and in fact the whole building was a dismal dark shade of black.

The Parish Priest was a Father Goss, very Dutch and large, who found English difficult. The one thing in his favour was that he could recite Mass in twenty- nine and a half minutes.

Dad would send us off on a Sunday morning with a pack of "snap" (sandwiches) and the order to attend Mass before eating them. On enduring this minor ordeal we (Bob and I) left church, mounted our one-gear bikes and headed for the hills. More specifically of course we headed with the Lloyd brothers to Tickhill (*beauty* (?)) and Worksop beyond.

A whole day of cycling and what we called "mucking about" or leaning over bridges looking at trout or grayling.

In my opinion Father Goss had an unfortunate name because it was close to a rather disgusting name for spit. In Yorkshire the offensive form of local spit was a thick mucus and very green. Most was expectorated on Saturday nights when the Public Houses turned out their customers. The past tense example "Ee spat on my front step" became "Ee gob bed on my front step". Gob is the Viking word for mouth and the phrase "Shut yer Gob" was frequently heard from quarrelling people.

Added to Father Gosse's attainments was his ability to produce a spray of fine globules when finding difficulties with his consonants; some vowels also gave articulation problems. On occasions we went with our parents to the eleven o'clock Mass and Bob and I sat underneath the pulpit. A strong light from the window illuminated the shower of particles descending in our direction and when Father was steamed up delivering a long and flowery sermon we boys lifted our shoulders, withdrew our heads and with collars as high as possible grinned and bore the storm.

We had five unmarried Aunts, all staunch Catholics. Any suitors were frowned on when they were young so they advanced in years as old maids. One, Ruth, did eventually marry and went to live in Surrey. Gertie and Mary ran a Boot and Shoe Shop and Agnes, the clever one, became a schoolmistress and was head of St. Bede's Junior School. She would insist on giving me extra Math's tuition but I told her after several weeks of torture that no longer would I accept it Arithmetic I loathed, though Brother Peter, at our Senior De La Salle College in Sheffield, taught me my tables and fractions. Algebra and theorems were a form of torture and quickly forgotten.

The Church organist was my Aunt Mary and for her years of service to the Organ the Pope sent her the Benemerenti Medal (This honour was established in 1832 and is awarded by the Pope for long and exceptional service to the Catholic Church). When very young I asked Aunty Mary why so many people came to church. "Souls for Heaven" she replied. The answer was to torment me for many years until I was mature enough to put the whole of this religious business into perspective.

Eventually Mother Nature had the last say and my belief in the miracle of nature predominated. To some friends would sign myself 'Fringy Druid', a Fringe Druid with thoughts of a meeting of like-minded people enjoying an annual gathering under an oak tree to praise Nature and all the gifts bestowed on us by her.

And Hadrian came to mind, who built a wall and a large temple in Rome named the Pantheon dedicated to all the known religions. In modern parlance he invited people to go in and choose for themselves and not to be envious or critical of other beliefs.

# Complete tolerance

We moved from Sherwood Crescent to a larger house in Clough Road, Masborough, still in Rotherham. The house was large with an extensive Attic. These upstairs rooms and especially the attic was an ideal studio for my Mother who painted mostly flowers, some landscape and portraits. We also had a table tennis table and spent happy hours there with Uncle Bert, an honorary Uncle, a steel maker with a local firm (he owned it!). An Uncle Louis put a large window in the roof to allow light in and florence was most pleased.

The move was a happy one as the large estate of Wentworth was only a couple of miles away. With Geof Lowe, my friend, we began to explore the whole estate and for many years it was our playground.

Camping was enjoyed and we put down our tents anywhere, no one objected in those days. Near to Greasebrough Village was a huge field called the Handkerchief Piece. It had the finest water welling up from a spring, and despite the gamekeeper's cottage being only a hundred yards away he never objected. There was also a stream near his house for bathing, underneath a waterfall! What joyous days they were.

# THE ROTHER

ROTHERHAM   1930

The Rother---gave it's name to Rotherham.

Of course the town was dirty

But now Jack the Peep, aged ten

Was afloat in a boat, Dad at the oars

And Mother safely wedged within

Thus our Jack could see mushrooming villas

Built by Steely men, Society's pillars

And one called Bert of Allott fame

Decides to join in this up-market game

But he said   'I'll have local men:

Earnshaw ee got brickies from Greaseborough

Men like Askey and Sykes, a couple of tykes

But strong : they'll build in Northants bricks and Barnsley stone

And 'Argreaves  he'll do t' doowers and floowers

Young Philip Smith in t'town square will furnish

And Banner Cox will garnish with paint

I've seen a lovely pair of chairs in Cox Dewar and

 Beaton  (which I'm told cum from a posh 'ouse in Seaton)'

 Now, enjoy a leap of ninety years

 And leaning on Chantrey Bridge

 (And all that time not a sign of a midge)

 But Mother Nature's cleaning up, and at last some

 Green can be seen, and to cap it all, a kingfisher has been seen

# Wentworth Woodhouse

Near Rotherham in Yorkshire is the estate of Wentworth *to which I have already alluded*. It was owned by Lord Fitzwilliam and is reputed to be the largest private house in England.

In my youth it was my playground and a major influence on my persona as it was a paradise of bird and wildlife. Birds especially; and with my friend Geof Lowe we covered almost every acre of that estate.

In the spring there were snipe skimming over the Fenton Fields and the numerous ponds were inhabited by newts and beautifully blotched salamanders. The lakes were extensive and cannot remember ever having to ask permission to camp, which we did regularly. Coots and moorhens nested there and often we had a fry up of their eggs.

A tree had fallen into the lake edge and over the years the water had grown through the tangle of branches. I watched a dabchick and located its nest - a mound of sodden growth. The mound extended above the water level; I swam out to examine this strange nest. There were white eggs with a shell, which was rough compared with the eggs of most other birds. And the nest was covered with debris - debris that covered the eggs - to avoid attention when the bird leaves according to my Kearton Bible.

Next the gamekeeper's cottage a refreshing waterfall - a most wonderful playground and the gamekeepers never objected.

# Wentworth: A Sketch Of The Estate.

The house out-bedroomed any large country house in England. As an apprentice decorator in the firm of Banner Cox, Percy St, Rotherham I was often given the task of painting walls and woodwork in the many guest rooms. One I remember well was titled the daffodil room (shades of Wordsworth!) What delight for a guest to be shown into such a sparkling billet

In the quiet of the painting session heard a scream and looking out of the window saw a rabbit transfixed by the mesmeric powers of an encircling stoat. I rushed down the steps and separated the now embroiled two animals. I dismissed the stoat and after giving the rabbit the punch to the back of the neck I was able to give my friend Len, who was working in another part of the building a free meal for his family.

# Scholes

Lord Fitzwilliam had a friend who was a Naval Architect The friend proposed that he could build a tower so high it would (from the top) enable his Lordship and friends to view the whole Estate.

It was duly built and to this day the tower dominates the area. The locals called it the Scholes Coppice, Scholes being the name of the Architect. The field next to it was excellent for camping and we naturally loved to rough it especially when the village had a fish and chip shop and a store where we could purchase a loaf and milk.

On one occasion we invited our two girl friends Gladys and Ruth, to camp next to us, and they duly arrived with borrowed bivouac and whatever on bicycles. They could cope with brewing up and cooking, as they were both practical girls.

Their tent was a little on the tatty side and as we, Geof and I, had adequate sleeping bags; we invited them to sleep with us. Our bags were large blankets, folded and sewn down one side, so it was a very prickly invitation. The girls agreed, however, and at sundown in their underclothes, they slithered in to our just enough room) bags.

Sleep was what we offered and sleep is what they got and of course we enjoyed their bodily warmth. No hanky-panky, and for several nights we enjoyed blissful exchange of heat. Long to be remembered as a very prickly but warm experience.

Fitzwilliam's pits covered acres of land. They were known as slag heaps and provided a challenge with their undulations for us young boys.

Our one-gear bikes enabled us to discover a large area of South Yorkshire and I well remember cycling through Wincobank between Rotherham and Sheffield accompanying my cousin Joan who went there for a dancing lesson. There were extensive banks on either side of the road and a full mile was covered with moon pennies or oxeye daisies. A white wonderland of flower and I was impressed!

Wentworth was a sporting estate and pheasants were bred for the shooting season.

In late April and May the gamekeepers scoured path fringes and lane edges where they knew the hen birds had their nests. An arduous and time filling occupation over a period of two or three weeks that had to coincide with the farm fowls going broody.

The estate carpenter provided the small coops that were about fourteen by fourteen inches wide. At one side was a sliding door that was lifted a few inches to allow the chicks to enquire into the outside world and find where they could be fed and watered. The broody hens having been collected from the farms were unceremoniously dumped on their clutch of eggs. There was no room to object and usually after an hour of clucking their objection and finding no way out they settled down to begin the period of hatching. There was nothing else they could do and quickly their mother instinct dominated.

After three weeks both chicks and mother were allowed about a square yard of earth and grass. The poults grew quickly and an ample supply of grain was given daily. At this stage the difficult bit arrived as the birds were allowed the run of a large pen in the woods. There they grew into adult birds and when three quarters grown were allowed more space still.

The gamekeepers' larder as it was called - a huge board which had nailed on it the corpses of vermin mostly stoats, weasels and birds of prey .......

The Scholes camping came to an end in 1938 and one minor triumph was the discovery of a whinchat's nest with four eggs in and found after a dedicated few hours of watching the birds.

Brother Columbus, I'm sure, was disappointed in me. But I comforted myself that although I was near bottom of the class no one else in my class had seen the nest of a whinchat with eggs!

In my book 'A Visual Journey' I wrote something about the old lifeboat purchased by my friends Geof Lowe and Philip Smith. It was complete but had been poorly repaired and had several minor holes.

In the summer of '38 the boat was brought from the Hull along the canal system and beached at Rotherham. Geof and I set to, to repair the damage, and after successfully plugging the faults I brought tins of surplus paint from the workshop where I was an apprentice (With Banners' permission of course). The paint was lead and gave the finest cover you could hope for. After two coats it was allowed to dry thoroughly and then given two coats of ship's varnish.

Later that year the Anti-Aircraft Unit called me up and it was to be several months before I met Geof again.

The lifeboat, he said, had been commandeered, fitted with an engine and took off dozens of soldiers stranded at Dunkirk! At least two journeys - our summer's work was a minor triumph!

# 1936 Rotherham

Behind Percy Street was a store
owned by Rothrum's top decorator Banner Cox
Monday and instructions sound thus:
To his staff in waiting: Billie and Jack
Take an andcart, load it wi lime and buckets
And tak a six foot ladder cos missus
Southgate's got a leaking cutter
    You knower she's opposite the Goose
    at Wickersley
A bit of a push I know, and don't get
wheel stuck in them tram lines
    tak a lever in case
she says er coatooks fell off
and er usban d's ammered in a four
inch nail. "That'l do nicely e says
but it wont: it's my turn to wail
I'm nut avin that!
So please Banner get your lads
to fix a new one! So said Banner
stop at ironmongers in Wellgate
buy a new one and sent bill to me so
whitewash cellars and see tut gutter
I'II say no more it's down ill
Comin back, so you should be eer
    by half past four.

*Jack Fieldhouse*

# My War

It began in 1937 and with talk of war I spoke to my friends the Lloyds, Jack, Geof and Derek. If we were to stay together I suggested that we joined the Artillery; an Anti Aircraft Unit was being formed at Wentworth. Lord Fitzwilliam had offered the use of his extensive stables as HQ for an Ack Ack unit.

With the exception of Derek we "signed on" and for a whole year we were to attend "drills" at Wentworth, which consisted of marching and the use of a rifle etc. Every week a 'drill' which involved walking the two miles to the stables.

Most of the recruits came from mining villages such as Wentworth, Fenton, Elsecar and Stubbin. Most of these mines are now defunct. However, late in 1938 we were called to the colours and moved to Heddon Airport near Hull, This airport was privately owned: the odd biplane or monoplane a reminder of the leisurely days of yore.

We had an old Naval gun - quite useless for our needs and our stay there lasted only a few weeks until we moved to ABC Coxhill on the South side of the Humber estuary in December 1937. Here we had heavy 4.5 anti-aircraft guns.

Drills were performed daily and I was trained as a predictor operator.

The system worked like this:

First a range finder latched onto the enemy bomber through GL or Radar and once fixed it was able to convey to the Predictor (a metal box with dials giving the relevant information on the height and speed of the enemy plane). It was my job to predict where the plane would be if it continued on its course and to give the guns the correct information about where the plane would be in about, say, ten seconds

The plane would then run into a barrage of fire from four guns firing simultaneously. It wasn't always accurate of course, but the dense barrage of fire must have been upsetting (to say the least) to the bomber crews because they turned their attention from bombing Hull and the port of Immingham, into trying to eliminate the Ack Ack guns.

My friend, Sergeant Major Crispin told me (why did he confide in me?) that a bomb had dropped onto a gun site a few miles away, killing the whole crew, adding "don't tell anyone; it would be bad for morale".

A few night's later (on duty by my predictor) I could hear a peculiar "swish swish" sound and a few seconds later a mortar bomb landed in a ditch about 80 yards away. The whole area erupted. We were lifted at least 2 feet off the ground. Mud spattered everywhere and our HQ, in a farmhouse nearby, was sliced in two. There were many casualties.

It took several hours to re-align guns and the predictor and range finder were dealt with fairly quickly.

The CO invited us to see the crater next day; it was big enough to accommodate a council house was my assessment at the time. Shreds of heavy parachute were found as souvenirs.

One plane was certainly shot down, a Dornier, dubbed the flying pencil. Brother Bob was sent to guard it to make sure locals might investigate and take mementos.

The bodies of the airmen were lying there in the wreckage and I thought of the families in Germany who would be getting a telegram about a life lost - another instance of misery for someone.

We were moved around the Midlands to harass German bombers targeting industrial cents. Most vividly was Sheffield where I was born and educated. We were bedded in at Pitsmoor on 3.7 Ack Ack guns and one day I remember so clearly. I was given a 24hour pass and went home to Rotherham only a few miles away. The sirens wailed early evening and by six o'clock the bombers were dropping incendiaries on both Rotherham and Sheffield.

I later learned that Aunt Agnes in St Anne's Road, with her neighbours, doused several incendiaries in the street and miraculously not a house was set alight otherwise they would have had high explosive bombs dropped on them too.

Although officially on leave till the next day I was determined to get back to Pitsmoor (and only half a mile from my Christian Brothers de la Salle college). Luckily I stopped a wagon going to Sheffield and the driver dropped me off at Brightside. I knew the area well as it was a stop I used before Sheffield to walk up the hill to school.

When I arrived at the gun site someone else had taken my job as predictor operator so I was a free agent in the hands of Sergeant Brown. He said that some of the shells landed had failed to detonate. I think there were three having failed over the past two hours of intense action and he wanted the shells removed to a crater some eighty yards away. His instructions were Yorkshire simple "Goo steddi lad" and he thought as I did, that any violent shaking might trigger an explosion.

I just concentrated on carrying this frightening load to a place of safety (for everyone else!) As I approached the crater there were bombs shrieking down and quite close. I flung myself into the crater, shell and all, and hoped for the best. A bomb came down only yards away, the explosion causing me to be partly covered in earth and shrapnel.

I lay there for a minute to thank the almighty that I was still alive and then went back for another. Subsequent journeys were by comparison quiet The raid came to an abrupt end about half past three and we all kipped down for a two-hour rest till reveille, breakfast and a quick march to bring back the circulation!

"Goo steddi" did the trick and all who had endured a night of action were pleased we had survived.

After a number of important area postings the time came when the Luftwaffe was reducing and the powers that be thought we might be more usefully used in North Africa.

We embarked at Liverpool and were to be conveyed in an American Liberty Ship. We headed out into the Atlantic to make our way by a devious route because of German U boats. It was an awful journey with rough seas and on the second night after being kept awake by depth charges dropped by a destroyer I tipped myself out of my hammock to go on deck.

Hard to believe what I saw. Alongside our troopship was the destroyer - our protector and the two captains were exchanging intelligence by megaphone.

Speech clear and decisive and I was so pleased to hear Harrovian articulation. I welled with pride and such dedication.

This reassuring exchange seemed to be coming from the best of our leadership and momentarily blessed the powers that be for two such men who had been nurtured and educated for this very moment.

We arrived at Tunis in clear water and the local Arab boys were amusing us by diving so cleanly for coins thrown in the water. On land the CO said we had a 20 mile walk to our billet. Our destination was a place called Maison Blanch!

By the half way mark most soldiers had drunk all the water in their bottles foolishly I thought mine was still full!

The officers were exasperated at the state of some of the soldiers but there was nothing for it but to carry on.

How the route march was completed I don't know, but complete it we did and arriving at the camp we were all given our mug of team. It was so hot and it refused to cool under the African sun. With lips blistered we eventually drank the precious liquid and settled down for a well-earned rest.

We moved to Sousee, South of Tunis and established our gun site in case German bombers intended to put the docks out of action.

The Luftwaffe did not appear, they were being reduced by our own growing strength in the air and most of it American. Lethargy and rest, so bathing was high on the Agenda.

Manna from Heaven! We were stationed next to an American food dump! And we hadn't seen a tin of peaches for years. Also ham and tinned fruit without end!

At night I went to find tinned ham and pears and met an American guard patrolling the compound. His instruction was clear "For Gawd's sake don't take a tin - take the whole crate!" The CO found out quickly enough as some men supported their stretcher like beds on crates of tins! They were soundly "ticked ofr" for lack of sensitivity - the least they could have done was hide the stuff!

No charges of theft were bought against us but the men were encouraged not to advertise their lack of sensitivity even in these outrageous circumstances.

The CO sent for me to tell me I was to go on a course dealing with Aircraft recognition and with some American buddies I was put on a train back to Algeria.

The train consisted mainly of cattle wagons, cleaned (was hardly my word) at sidings by Mustafah and an Apprentice with a brush. Buckets of precious water swilled the floor and the cow muck brushed out It was, as were the rest of the wagons, a haven for flies.

The dry boards were where we slept - ground sheet and one blanket.

The CO had failed to tell us that the wagon was bugged - in modern parlance it has a definite wording but in the case of our "room", it had a different meaning, which anyone with Druid sympathies would easily understand.

And bugged it was and quite soon on the journey I developed (in subtle Army phraseology) a dose of Delhi belly.

The Viking word is "squits" which is much more descriptive. It wasn't a corridor train - they hadn't been invented then - ??? Without facilities I had to behave like a steer and as we trundled along there was nothing for it but to examine the door to find any ironwork that I would cling onto. There were handles and what a blessing!

I remember being so weak [ could hardly hang on but if I was to survive I had to hold and stick my backside out as far as it was possible so to do! This ghastly affliction subsided within a day and at one siding there was a reservoir in which I bathed luxuriously!

The campsite reached, we settled into normal routine and attended lectures. Most of this information I had had and ....... lectures on recognition. However it was a change of scene and my American friends were most affable so we got on well.

We were moved by American troop ship to Naples - the Italian campaign was increasing in momentum and we were installed in an area in central Italy for Infantry training.

An Italian woman takes away 1 cwt of mule manure to her garden some 100 yds away!

Jack Fieldhouse

It was at this stage that I was seconded to a Muleteer group for carrying ammo and stores to an Infantry Unit high in the mountains of Central Italy. The work, if it can be called work, was to take Jacko, my mule on a journey, which took the whole day along the most difficult of stony paths. Jacko the Mule, if allowed to get his head down for a blade of grass was difficult to move and it took all my strength to lift his head and move on. And I soon discovered that the essential qualification as a Muleteer was to be able to remove a stone splinter from the hoof of the animal.

If Jacko was limping, I had to treat the afflicted area and with soothing tone work my hand over the leg and then quickly grab the leg and lift it. Fortunately I had the strength to hang on as Jacko struggled to get rid of me.

With my 1914-18 Army knife, which had a sharp projection blade, I was able to find and remove the offending impediment At the end of a trying day, and on returning to the village, Jacko refused to move beyond the apple stall. It was not until we had bought apples and fed the wretched animal that we were able to move on!

The Mules were stabled and produced manure; the Italian women, the lightly older ones with gardens would take all the manure produced. They had large sheets and the manure was swept on to the centre and then it would take four strong soldiers to lift it (suitably tied of course) on to the back of one of these women, the contents oozing a watery filth all over their backs and hair!

Once the load was steadied (and I can see now the shift of the legs to ensure that the weight was distributed evenly) this fearsome female would stagger off to her garden with the precious load. These people survived on their garden produce and rabbit meat so anything to encourage fertility was seized upon.

At Wesenan there was a mountain stream full of trout. The two hooks I had been carrying in my wallet for this occasion were brought out and with a yard of line (also brought) I fixed myself up with a wand from some hedge and the arrangements worked well. I had no reel and when trout was caught I simply lifted it out onto the bank.

No artificial flies, I caught all my fish on moths, bluebottles, earwigs or any insect that would continue to wriggle when impaled on a hook: the cooks were pleased and the Officer's Mess were grateful.

Our next move was to Unter Stelmark close to the Yugoslavian border. The people there had been under Russian rule for several years and they still had to manage largely on what the countryside could provide.

At the first opportunity I set off to look at a village in the hills. I cut myself a stick and set off. Within an hour I was there and found the place ominously quiet. I walked along the main street - just houses of wood on either side. There wasn't a soul about - at least that was my first impression. Then - a face peering at me from behind a house.

Then another and yet another and they must have decided somehow that I wasn't a threat and suddenly I was surrounded by women and girls. An extraordinary atmosphere - there wasn't a sound except for surrounding feet. They stopped as though by a signal. From the midst of these faces a girl spoke: 'Where are your guns?'

Naturally I was taken aback as I was standing there in shorts and shirt tucked in and carrying a stick! I showed the stick to assure them that was all I carried. For years Russian soldiers had cowed them and they always carried pistols or guns.

I had the feeling that they couldn't believe that this single Englishman could suddenly appear amongst them unarmed. I was made most welcome and they asked me to visit them again.

From Martyuschlag with a friend and borrowed bikes we spent the night there. We were provided for with slices of pig lard (and salt!) Delicious and I have never ceased to wander about these people - no men, they had been sent off to work in factories somewhere in Russia.

Probably at that moment a chink of light was allowed to see the future as the war had ended and the political situation should be allowing the return of their loved ones and that one day the heart of their great city of Vienna might beat again.

A daily pint of milk and I remember a ration of bread being issued (in Vienna.) We went there on a bitterly cold weekend and apart from the deprivation of the populace they managed without light or heat It's hard to imagine how they coped but there must have been a black market in foodstuffs from the countryside and communal cooking provisions.

However they did survive by virtue of their common sense and cooperation.

A night billet in a hospital and floors were liberally covered with DDT and the bed paillasses on iron beds had been stored in corridors when the Russians left. They were infested with bed bugs. It took me four days of intense searching to rid myself of these creatures - they were so persistent and very often I woke up bleeding from their midnight blood feasting.

With winter approaching we were moved to a most dreadful billet in the mountains, a hamlet called Gullrad, where I was told the son of a local prince was out hunting and met a local girl with whom he fell in love. A social dieback ensued and I don't know what happened so why am I writing it?!

Gullrad, in the winter was a playground for sledging - the road of packed ice and snow was ideal for attaining high speeds on their superbly made toboggans.

The Forester lived in the house next to our billet, which was the guesthouse. He was the gamekeeper of the extensive forest and invited me to a day's shooting. His instructions were clear: You shoot Father, Mother, Aunt, Cousins! In other words if I had the chance to shoot any deer I was to take it!

Food was important with severe rationing and a carcass would be shared with the whole village. He and his wife were a generous couple and he was delighted to play a humorous trick on his wife with Colman's mustard! Never had he had mustard with such a sting.

His son was a doctor and he had an impressionable 16-year-old daughter who was increasingly casting a motherly eye in my direction.

Came the Spring and warmer weather and all the stock within the capacious barn ventured out to enjoy the warmer days.

About mid-March the CO came to see me to say that my de-mob papers had come through_Our unit possessed a vehicle called a "caterpillar" similar in design to a small tank, the tracks designed for snow. We had a choice: to risk going over the Pass with this vehicle carrying our luggage and we walking; or waiting a few weeks for the warmer weather and the avalanche threat receding.

We chose to walk it and off we set on this hazardous trek of several miles and at times the going was difficult for our tractor and we had to push.

At the north end of the Pass we said goodbye to the tractor and driver and from then on we headed to some railway terminal in an army truck.

The journey through France was tedious and most uncomfortable and to gain any idea of the interior of these French wagons one can do no better than to study some of the drawings of Honore Daumier. His observations on a troisieme classe give you a clear idea of the wooden seats and backrests that passengers had to endure.

A channel port was reached, which seemed to be inhabited by Tarty French girls (Tarts) on the look out for customers.

With Blighty in sight we made the trip home and to Aldershot busy with de-mob papers and questioning officials.

# Instances

An afternoon at Studland Bay near Bournemouth

Suddenly an alarm - man the guns! We raced for our 3.7 Anti Aircraft guns from our bivouacs.

The Bofers ('?)were already in action pounding away at an incoming plane. It was low and an easy target. Badly holed it came down in the sea and luckily the pilot was unscathed. Someone had boobed as we normally got a warning from our Radar system.

Unidentified the plane was assumed to be a German. Whoever identified it do so wrongly. It was a Spitfire with floats. What monstrous carelessness! However the airman was OK but very lucky.

A command fault but it must have been in the minds of those gunners that recently the Messerschmit 110 had flown so low the Radar didn't pick it up and it came in unmolested and fired a volley of machine gun fire into the marquee where with others I was taking breakfast.

Some slight excuse I thought for the confusion of the moment.

# Mrs Oglesby and Mablethorpe

In Yorkshire parlance Mrs Oglesby was "chuffed off" with her menfolk. They lived in Clough Rd., Masbro almost opposite to the Fieldhouses.

All these houses were substantial and built for high earners: the main idea was that the front rooms of all these houses could accommodate the coming craze of "Billiards".

So, in the case of the Oglesby's their capacious front room had a state-of-the-art billiard table.

There were famous names which dominated this game, and with it the beginning of a new phase in wireless - the running commentary.

Mrs Oglesby was there to provide meals and drinks to both Mr Oglesby and his brother who lived with them

These two men worked at the foundry at the end of Clough Road and could be likened to a pair of Zombies.

They ate in silence at the evening meal- a necessary function, with staring eyes and no conversation. At the end of the meal they left the dining room for the billiard room when they settled down to the only think that meant anything in their lives. And on till bed time when they reluctantly had to come to a full stop.

Mrs Oglesby enduring this Zombie-like existence, saved up as much as she could out of the housekeeping and once a year hired a large Vauxhall car and went off with her two boys (one old enough to drive) to Mablethorpe and into a caravan and peace!

Jack and Bob Fieldhouse were invited and we all piled into this large car driven by the eldest boy of some eighteen years.

A very dicey journey but fortunately next to no traffic on the roads and before the driving license had been thought of. Instructors were people who owned a car, had driven reasonably well and could certainly give life-saving tips on steering.

Mrs Oglesby had picked up a book on the Egyptians and had read that the Dynasty of the CUTNAK produced a ruler who loved the sound of little boys with falsetto voices. Later in history this was to become the castrata practise which improved the singing voice of young males.

They invented this game of balls (ivory) and straight sticks on a flat furface which developed into the billiard table of today.

Eventually they devised pockets and the law of breaks when balls had to be bounced off one ball and go into the said pocket.

The Zombies came into being!

Mrs Oglesby searches in the shallows for her false teeth! Help coming!

Mrs Oglesby looking $\frac{3}{4}$ - dejected after having lost her false teeth (washed out by a wave)

# Mablethorpe

Having left her menfolk to cater for themselves - mainly of fish and chips, the holiday home came into view.

Nothing extraordinary with crude beds and cooker heated by gas. The loo was a shed reached by a wooden bridge (two planks and a handrail). One had to walk the plank to get to it: it was the foulest of cabins with a primitive seat over a deep hole. The stench was almost unbearable but somehow we got through the week without contracting some deadly disease.

Amusements? Near the beach a kiosk with hats and lettering on the front ie "Kiss me Quick" for the girls. Nothing for the boys except rock which had MAB through the middle and I suspect that the confectioner got so far and decided that the whole of 'Mablehorpe' couldn't be suckable and that is all that mattered.

For Mrs Oglesby cooking and a book and the occasional walk along the sand to the beach. A disastrous occasion towards the end of the week - she went in for a bathe: a wave came and unbalanced her: she emitted a loud hoop-Ia and she lost her false teeth.

Poor Mrs Og. trying to locate them and joined by children with their shrimp nets to help in the search.

The poor woman had to remain toothless 'till her return to Rotherham.

The Outside Loo & Stable In32 B
(A Mother & Children) (The Smallies)

# My dear friend Frank Morris

Frank Morris I must mention. He was a close friend for many years while he was I/C financial affairs at County Hall, Taunton.

He wrote a Country Column for the Somerset Gazette for many years and on my retirement from Priory Boys he asked me to take over, which I did.

Frank was a brilliant fisherman and a good shot so that many a Saturday we would go off rabbiting or 'rough shooting' with a spaniel borrowed from my farmer friend, Ken Webber.

The spaniel was completely untrained and would go racing ahead and sometimes to our advantage. A pheasant flushed sometimes flew right over us and one gun or the other would put it in the 'bag'.

Frank knew the controller of farms owned by the council so we had memorable pigeon 'bags' when birds were flying into roost in the evening.

We had a large sack for the occasion and when filled with about 20 birds it was a heavy load to carry back to our vehicles.

One interesting article Frank wrote of in his weekly column was he and his wife Hilda were invited to a wedding. Frank knew that the reception would be on a spacious lawn and a trout stream next door. Frank couldn't resist sneaking his rod in the car!

Boring Gudergies - Frank sneaked off to try and caste in this tempting water, tiptoeing away and not really taking care of what was underfoot tripped and fell headlong into the water. He had to present himself to the heartless guests with much laughter and an ignominious retreat home.

# Lynmouth (Foul Hooked Mackeral)

The family often had a week in a friends' cottage at Bridgeball about a mile upstream from Lynmouth.

A hot July and I was walking on the very pebbly beach at Lyton.

The local council thought it would be a splendid idea to make a concrete swimming pool on the beach.

High tide would fill it and bathers would not have to negotiate rocks and pebbles in order to get into deep water for a bathe. For children it was impossible.

The concrete bathing pool was duly made and on this hot August day with Martin my son we went to look.

The pool was full of water and hundreds of mackerel too!

By hook or by crook I thought I'm going to fish out some of those. Martin was told – " go to the van and bring my fishing tackle"

Very quickly it arrived and for the last six foot of line I put hooks

When the hooks had been fastened (there were some ten of them spaced out about one every eight inches). I told Martin to drive the fish across the deep end of the pool and as they crowded past my line I gave a vigorous upward jerk which foul-hooked two or three every drive.

In a matter of ten minutes we had about two dozen fish and at that point we decided to stop as there were too many close onlookers who presented a danger.

Fish for us and neighbours and a memorable hours 'foul hooking'!

# Grindleford

To some the piece of music entitled 'In a Monastery Garden' might be seen as an over sentimental piece but to me as a ten year old (or younger) it was the most delightful of sounds.

A hot August day in Derbyshire and for the best of the day I had been fishing in the Derwent for Sticklebacks. I had caught a red-bum the name we gave to the male stickleback in this condition I was sent off with a sandwich and a two pound jar with string round the rim for carrying

Returning for lunch about three pm, barefoot and enjoying the sensation of walking on a pavement of warmer slate, I suddenly encountered a sound coming from a cottage window. A most delightful music which prompted me to sit and listen It was "In a Monastery Garden". And I concentrated on every note. And ever since I have enjoyed it, and was a comfort to me on some of my darkest days.

At Grindleford Mother was never short of eggs. The local farm had fields fenced in by high wooded stakes and cross bars. Nettles and weeds grew around the base of these posts. The farm hens loved this situation and layed their stray eggs under this concealing mass of growth.

Jack was very adept at finding nests and had no compunction about taking the eggs!!

Mistances The Egg?

Jack searching for stray eggs

# Priory Boys

At Priory Boys. Taunton their names gave a clue to their origins. The names Fouracre and Fower Acker show an insight into some families and they should suffice.

The Fouracres were modern and advanced to the point where their name was more sociably acceptable but still a good name, whereas the Fower Acker group revelled in their rural and rooty beginnings where Four acres was the area of land on which a family could sustain themselves.

The school enjoyed the usual aberrations which are bestowed on most schools.

There was, for example, a moment when a caretaker spoke rudely to a boy who in turn made life difficult for the said caretaker by shoving bog rolls down the toilet (or should it have been 'bug'!

The headmaster withdrew all toilet rolls and issued them to each class teacher to bestow on any pupil the appropriate sheets for the occasion.

I, with great flourish, would say 'One for the main job', second sheet for cleaning up the area concerned and a third for a polish.

Oddly this intimidating experience put an end to the practise within a week!

I watched two boys (they hadn't seen me) standing on dustbins and every boy who came round the corner was spat upon.

I could have marched them to the headmaster for a good dressing down but instead just waited for the ammunition to come to an end: I called them 'Her Majesty's Expectorates'

Fortunately these moments were infrequent and the work of this excellent Secondary Modern School went on.

There were and always will be the misfits and we have to cope somehow.

The Staff were brilliant with plenty of humour and fairness to pupils under a most sensible and wholesome Paddy West – the Headmaster.

# Colonsay Island

With a party of boys from Priory Boys School, Taunton we set out for Colonsay Island at the beginning of the summer holidays.

We hired a Ford Van which took three masters: David Christie, Fred Brennand, Michael Derrick and me.

We took turns to drive and the first stop was Oban.

From there a Ferry to Colonsay. Not a long journey the Island appearing as a long slither of land in the distance.

Approaching the Harbour I heard a bird which by a process of elimination, was a Ringed Plover.

The Kearton Brothers had taught me well and I beckoned several boys who I knew were keen bird watchers, and told them that there was a Ringed Plover's nest to see once we had embarked.

I pointed out that the shore line consisted of pebbles right up to the point beyond them where grass grew.

The current summer high tide mark was where wrack brought in by the tide was deposited. The Plover well versed in water hazards and the dangers of predatory gulls make a shallow scrape within the pebbles and laid her eggs.

"Look between the wrack and grass" I told them. A short space only, and sure enough when reaching the area I found the nest which contained four eggs. Perfect camouflage and with the likelyhood of survival.

## Road mending Colonsay

Someone in Europe, more precisely the European Parliament realised that the Islands off Scotland were being neglected and money was paramount for updating these neglected communities.

The roads needed resurfacing and one August when we arrived with boys for a camping week, a large lorry load of stones and tar arrived and was dumped near the dock area of Colonsay.

It wasn't really a mound it was somewhat elongated and having deposited the load it awaited a machine for spreading it and a roller to boot.

After two days all the sheep on the island descended on this lovely warm pile of tar and stones.

It was ideal for a good nights kip thought the sheep.

When they got up to graze in the morning every animal had plumbobs of tar and stones attached. The shepherd's crop of wool was eliminated. What a mess.

# An Italian moment from Italy

An afterthought.

I was doubtful about setting this down as it was an account of a rather bizarre encounter in an area somewhere west of the Pontine Marshes and an area almost impossible to conduct any military manoeuvre. It therefore became a vast area with no military activity except that it was cautiously patrolled by both sides.

We were training on the southern edge of this area and some intelligence had come our way that a few miles away there were fifth columnists living in an old farm house. Captain Shuter asked me if I would go and investigate, so with Bill Kendrick (the Boxer) we set out to try to locate this isolated farm house and with the possibility of bringing back a prisoner.

The situation was described and we realised that we might not find it, but after being equipped with pistols and a torch we set off.

The *going* was tough as we had either to climb up terraced gardens or lower ourselves down steep slopes. Remarkably we found this farmhouse in a shallow valley: it was tall and as we approached it seemed deserted. And so it was, and the main door was easily opened which led into a staircase which was-

Very steep and very rickerty and I felt the need to test every step. I said to Bill that I would go first and on reaching the first floor there was no noise or signs of occupation.

The second floor was the same so I ascended to the third. Although I was as quiet as I could be I gained the third floor without opposition and pushed open the first door in front of me.

There was a sound of some sort and as I pushed open the door, and in my most authoratative voice said "Hende Hoche" spelling probably wrong, but I hoped my assertive tone *would* do the trick.

There were no humans and my light from the torch shone in the face of 'A Cow'.

Unbelievable that some locals knowing the value of such a beast should cajole, and with roped and pushing managed to get it up a rickerty staircase.

Bless 'em I thought and they had the daily task of feeding and watering the animal.

Milk for several families? What stoicism! - hard to believe but when needed must these people that they might come through to the end of the war by their dedication.

We departed without prisoners and we had no need to use our pistols and I'm sure had the need arisen we would have been dead men.

So lucky and in the early hours we were back to 'kip' down for a couple of hours of well earned rest.

# The Egg of the Sparrow.

When I was young in the 20's the sparrow was a common bird, its chirping could be heard in every backyard or garden in the country.

My father told me of the sparrow pies they had about the turn of the century. In my father's case he kept an eye on sparrow roosts invariably old walls where ivy grew upwards and outwards and which were ideal for a warm nights rest.

The procedure was simple but required stealth as all birds when disturbed will panic and fly out into the night air without considering where they will go.

A net was carefully lowered from the top of the wall by two or more individuals teasing it out in silence and when the net covered the whole of the roosting area the birds were duly panicked and flew out when they were caught. The top edge of the net was then quickly dropped down to waiting hands and then the birds enveloped were caught and killed.

A few dozen birds then had to be plucked and taken to the kitchen.

The plump birds made a good meal.

My egg collection included sparrows but I was always on the look out for more specimens as they varied from lightly covered black spots to heavily blotched ones. The sparrow egg I considered was one of the most beautiful in my collection.

One old sandstone barn always gave me the opportunity to add to my collection and I had no compunction to take ali could as they were so numerous.

The old barn in question was situated on a farm between Greaseborough and Masbro where I lived.

The important observation was to make sure the farm worker employed by the farmer wasn't around. And if he was absent I approached the barn with Indian expertise which involved cutting a wand from a Hawthorn about 2 ft long with plenty of tines (thorny outgrowths which protects the plant from depredation.

This barn was carelessly constructed or the blocks were intentionally left with goodly air spaces between for cooling and aerating crops within.

The sparrows love such spaces and quickly I could find an entrance because of the Sparrows carelessness when dragging hay or whatever into the nest area. At this juncture I must say something about a sparrows nest. It is quite unlike the nest of any other bird which uses grass, moss, feathers and the like. Put plainly it is a mess and is just an accumulation of rubbish.

This mess is easily extracted by inserting the thorny wand and rotating it. In contact with this untidy accumulation the wand grips it and by turning more and more, a considerable wedge of this material can be dragged out. And somewhere in the middle the sparrows eggs can be found. I feel sure that there is a semblance of a warm centre, but have never found it.

With care the eggs can be found, and I never had any qualms of conscience about taking all the eggs. It would have been impossible to shove them back anyway!

Was Barney about? Sometimes he would holler "Bugger off you boys"! and we would quickly do a Yorkshire "Skiddadle".

# The price of honey

It was August and after a good summer there was honey on my hives.

Jack has a plot of ground about a quarter of a mile from his house across a field. There were five beehives each with three supers of honey boxes.

Most were full and my method of removing the honey was primaeval - I simply took off the top two boxes leaving the one over the brood box which would contain over thirty pounds of honey; all this would be used to feed a new generation of bees the following year.

Each super has ten frames which are moveable, the bees make wax in each and then fill with honey. Each cell is then capped with wax which keeps the honey fresh.

On the occasion of this honey crop the same rules applied.

Each box lifted was put onto an empty box and with plenty of smoke from my smoker (an essential tool for this particular job), each frame covered with bees were brushed clean and the new frame of honey was put into a separate box and covered with a cloth.

This prevented bees from re-entering.

When my veil touched my neck or face the bees were able to sting.

The process took at least an hour and my farmer friend Ken Webber had loaned me his light van to enable me to take off the crop.

It had been raining and the way out was a 60 yard slope to a flat field. About half way I found that ere was only one way out: each box had to be taken off and carried twenty yards through a gate and into the flat field.

Hundreds of bees tried to gain access to what was their honey.

Speed was essential and twelve heavy honey boxes were moved to the field and covered to prevent robbing!

The van then lighter, by a bit of readjusting gripped the sod and emerged through the gate where the boxes had to be reloaded.

With stings too numerous I made it home and put the crop into my honey extracting shed.

Sweat and stings but almost a cwt of delicious honey!

# A Romantic Tale

As I said we had seven children and one Julie my third daughter came to the Island of Colonsay with my friends David Christie and Fred Brennand and with a party of boys from Priory Boys from Taunton Priory Boys School.

We hired a large Ford van and off we set at the beginning of the summer holiday and by kind permission of Lady Grathcona we tented on the Colonsay House Lawn "The kitchen window you can lift and turn on the tap for hot water" - she said, and in return we cut back a lot of the overgrown escallonia by the drive. The poor postman found it difficult to approach the house!

Colonsay is an island to the south of Colonsay where the McNeils live in a large farmhouse.

One day my daughter Julie and her friend Rita who in a way was adopted by us because her brothers and sisters were so much older than she, set off to cross the mile wide strand and covered by the tide twice in 24 hours.

The tide was low and just about to change and they had been warned that after a slog of one mile with the tide coming they would be literally in deep water.

They stripped off and bundling their clothes (sleeves make useful ropes), they set off carrying all on their heads. They were wading in deep water as they approached the shore.

They made for the McNeil's house and after almost a mile found a remote cottage and a man on the roof apparently doing some repairs.

This man was the Art Master of Wellington College working for his friend whose father rented tt:)e grazing on the Island.

The cottage was called Seal Cottage and when Jason saw Julie his fate was 'sealed'.

They met at various Cedilh's - I prefer the phonetic 'Kay Lee' and later that year were married.

Jason applied for the job of in charge of the Art Department Harrow School. He was in complete charge of employing assistants and even before living at the school had to advertise and interview. Quite a post and we visited them on several occasions: Concerts - I remember Feure and Durufle and the Chinese boys in the orchestra. Julie remarked on their industry and commitment!

Access to the library too and on one occasion the librarian would like to read some essays on war by a teenager. They were incredibly graphic accounts of battles, the men, officers and strategy. Such vision! And yes, they were by one 'boy' Winston Churchill who I was told when he was disruptive was sent out of the room to sit on the stairs with - a dictionary!

# A Sleepless Night

At Colon say I had made up my mind to paint a picture of the large house owned and lived in by the McNeils.

The house was on Oronsay, so with a haversack in which all gear was stored I set off to walk the mile wide strand. Basic stuff only - a small board, palette a bag of paints, oil and turps and brushes.

It was summer but with an east wind a bit on the cool side. With the tide low I was able to make good progress and I first of all called to see the McNeils.

I was offered coffee and clouty dumpling! Now this bread/cake was heavy and filled with fruit and most indigestible except for the natives!

I left mine hosts to find ground where I could squat and sketch. It was cool and I attracted several sheep whose sole purpose was to obscure the view.

With effort I produced a sketch and stored everything back into my haversack.

Arriving at the shore line the tide was going out, but the water over a foot deep,l so I waded and as I reached the shore on the Colonsay side the water had receded and there waiting for me was Martin and a couple of boys.

It was cold and the east wind had induced an overpowering thirst.

On to the newly opened cafe by the harbour where I ordered a pint of hot coffee well sugared with a table spoon.

That night I didn't sleep a wink!

In future I thought water or a soft drink, but coffee NO.

# Lundy Island

One late summers day we took our friend Bob Banfield to Lundy Island.

Our boat was the APT a twenty footer. Wet storm petrels on the way and disembarked into almost 3 ft. of water to go ashore. There was not a landing platform in those days.

Thoroughly wet to the waist we struggled ashore.

Joan's intention was to see the wild goats the offspring of survivors from a wrecked Spanish ship which ran aground.

She was lucky enough to see some.

Bob Banfield enjoyed looking at the village and I went for a walk to the end of the Island.

At some high point on my return I stood and looked out to sea and saw one of the most outstanding of sights: Suddenly a square mile of ocean 'shimmered' and my estimate was that a million mackerel came to the surface where they turned with a flourish their sides reflecting the light of day.

Within two seconds it was all over. Some hidden order they obeyed: can you imagine a Mistress Mac saying 'When I say go you flip on the surface' and they all obeyed and the same with the other side. I called it *joi de vivre*!

Never have I seen anything like it, and it was a wonderful experience.

The way back was horrendous with choppy waters caused by a heavy tide coming round the Island. It bucketed down with rain and the water cascaded down the sail onto the huddled passengers.

We were drenched and my wife insisted that our friend Bob Banfield strip off and huddle under a blanket (always carried for such occasions).

# A Hospital Visit

I poked my nose into one of the rooms in Bridgwater Hospital. Several old folks in there and a great feeling of expectancy!!

On the river Parrett below the the window was a floating feet up. Somewhere upstream it had drowned! Poor thing floating by and Mavis says that when the tide turns it will come back again.!!

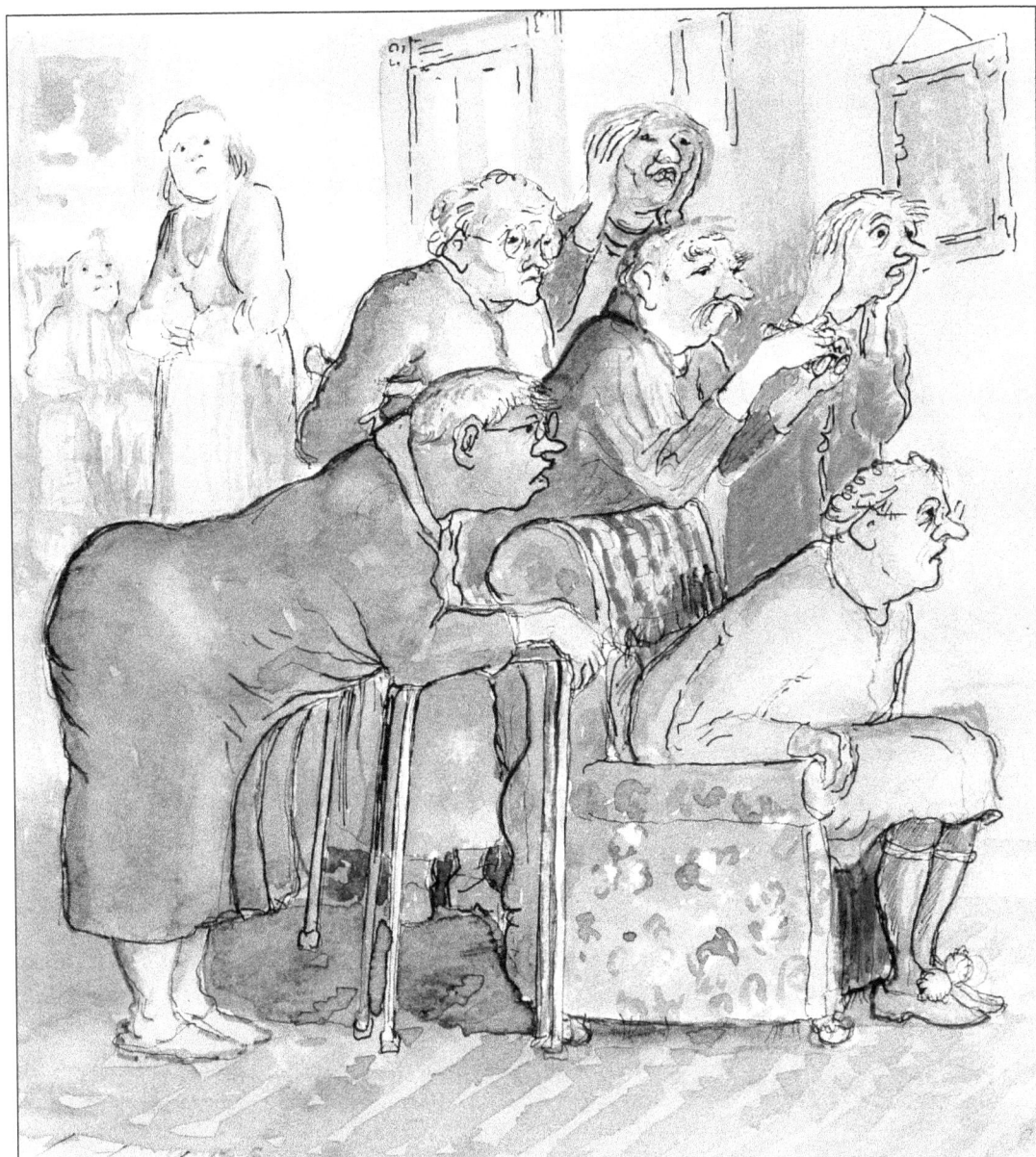

The Mary Stanley Incident !
Mavis says that when the Tide J. Fieldhouse
turns it will come back again !

Through the hospital window the old folks
observe a dead cow going out with the tide
(The Parrett is a tidal river) and Mavis
says that when the tide turns it will come
back again !

J.Fieldhouse   2001

# Instances – The Hen

In the days of Yore, you could find an egg on any barn floor
And everywhere, unregulated hens would lay
 Some high up in unceremouniously dumped stooks of hay
Came war and rationing and a Govermental decree said birds should have a sheltered life
In properly build sheds away from strife
Wire floors for eggs to roll
So chickies do not be afraid
You will have corn and grit, and a boring day
So long as you have an egg to lay
But soon the dominating lunnes said CRUEL
The birds need space and a dust renewal
The time of Antis had arrived!
Meanwhile cunning Jack bought three juvenile layers
Which by Christmas day proved to be stayers
Three eggs a day appeared
Begon you Govermental eggs!
Your days are over, at last we peg
Our hopes on more and our friends can come
For tea and a boiled
Full praise then for the hen
*Amen*

# In recognition

So many people I have been privileged to have met or known more closely.

Thanks to my first friend Connie Atkinson for my first 'anatommy' lesson at a very early age

To the Fitzwilliams for their vast estate where with friends I camped, swam in the lakes and helped myself to clutches of moorhens eggs, which were fried for breakfast.

To lady Fitzwilliam whilst I decorated the Daffodil room took me by the hand and showed me portraits of the family.

And to another lady (again by the hand) who showed and explained her exhibition of paintings in a large house in Rotherham.

Her name was Ethel Walker (Dame) and the house in Rotherham had extensive grounds, which later became Clifton Park and the large house Clifton Museum.

The Walkers had lived there in the past before moving to Liverpool where they founded the Liverpool Art Gallery

To the men I served with when joining the Anti Aircraft unit at Wentworth.

Fine men and completely reliable – men from the villages (mining) near Wentworth of Stubbin, Elsecar, Scholes and Greaseborough.

To my parents, dad a chemist in Steel and my mother who taught me a lot about painting.

And so many Army friends who endured a bitterly cold winter near the Humber Estuary, relieved by the hours of action against German Bombers.

And just a few words about my anticedents: My father had a Great great Grandmother who as a young lady rebelled against the strictness of her family the Percys who live in Northumberland. She came South and married a butcher at Ilkley. He passed on his genes to my father who kindly passed them on to me.

Interestingly, these old familie produce odd or outstandingly difficult personalities at times. The Percy family had one bright light – Guy Fawkes.

Musn't forget my Gladys Williams. We attended Art school together at Rotherham: We went for long walks, rested on the brightly coloured Poa Grass in Fenton Woods.

A wonderful teenage friendship Art and Kisses.

Outstanding people who give pleasure by their company! Will name Two at least: my editor Fisha Morris and lovely daughter Alice From Trisha a compliment – my script needed little alteration – she liked my Yorkshireisms!

# Glastonbury 2013

Benfath a Glastonbury moon
Lies a city of bodies and soon
The worthy cock his voice
Attuned to waking five ( and if he's to stay alive )
He has no choice but to fling his chanticleery sound
To every tend and bivouacy mound
His message is awake, you hairy lot!
And queue to wash and find a coloured sit-a-pot
And busy girls with tresses dangling too near the fire
Make brekker burgers, Oh my, Oh my!!
With fingers hot and greasy
( A backside rubbing cleans them easy!)
And soon the walk about begins
A sight to see!
A buttocky morning with knobbly knees
But clean well aired
And busoms enjoying a Glastonbury freedom
And loving glances, no sign of ranter
And a full day of banter, fizzy pop and all
And faces saying give us more
Dear Elvis, we do implore
So hold your magic stick
Wave it and promis to perform the trick
Of lifting hearts, by saying Yes
To another madness at Pilton Green
Next june in twenty thirteen

*Madaline at Glastonbury has found a spiritual experience prompted by
a high backed wicker chair. For a moment, perfect piece*

Jemima gesticulates
at Glastonbury

JF 2011

Flowers at Glastonbury. 2011

Gorgeous
Glastonbury

Gorgeously Glaston

J Fieldhouse
2012

Isla brings the Sugar (Glastonbury 2011
Jack Fieldhouse

Isla is the wife of Hamish the Druid.
Very athletic she prefers to leap over the door
rather than to open it

ica love
[illegible] love
huy

A Gooey
Gooey
moment!

An airma
GlasTonbur
busoms
2013

J.F.

GLASTONBURY

AN ENDEARING TRAIT — SHOWING KINDNESS
TO ANIMALS — here feeding the birds!

The 'false'
Flamingos!

Glastonbury 2011.        Jack Fieldshow

Glastonbury

Maeve Jo & Lucy

J.F.

in the Tree House
99.

# Post War: Marriage And Family

From there home and as I had decided not to go back to Rotherham till there were salmon in the River Don I moved in with an Aunt (Ruth) who lived in Woking.

I took a job as a decorator for a few weeks and then decided I might try to resume my Art studies (I had had a year at the Rotherham School of Art before the war) so went to Guildford where I was accepted and was given a small bursary.

Came the Autumn and a farmer from Cambridgeshire needed hands to pick his apples. I thought a week of activity would be a good idea so I volunteered. Housing and meals free, so off I went. On the train and a comely wench standing in the corridor attracted me.

Arriving at the camp (Wisbeach?) she was still there and on the first day picking we agreed to help together.

I did the gentlemanly thing and offered to steady the ladder while she climbed for the fruit. It was simple - the apple was picked and thrown down to outstretched arms and hands.

I was in a good position to see more of her legs than the usual from the knee downwards. They looked strong and marriageable so when she came down I proposed to her and she accepted. We were married in the December!

We began married life in a house in Old Woking belonging to my Aunt Ruth with whom I had been living for the past three years.

London University for a whole year and then a post of Art Master at a school in Bridgwater.

Five years there and then to a boys' only comprehensive in Taunton where I stayed for another seventeen years. On leaving I refused a clock and said I would prefer a sledgehammer and a wedge.

Dutch Elm disease was rife at the time and a large quantity of wood came my way - very knotty and it required great effort to reduce it.

However it was a great source of cheap fuel and kept the home fires burning and my wife Joan cooking for several years.

We had seven children and all except one are professional. The 'one' is Duncan who as a child was inoculated with something (against some disease) and it affected his brain.

Now as I write he is fifty years old and a happy boy who goes for long walks (comes in at worrying late hours sometimes.) He is very strong - hefts loads of coal and collects wood on his walk. He is a gem and so good-natured.

He is the major sorrow in our lives. There have been others; young Derek Lloyd who at the time when war was coming I hoped would join us by enlisting in the Ack Ack battery at Wentworth. Derek - a shining face with his Maths and the Architects bible clutched in his hand - the Bannister Fletcher which encompasses all the styles in European Architecture.

Derek was called up and was sent to an infantry unit where he lost his life in a hail of bullets somewhere near Carthage in North Africa. We were at Sousse and the CO a thoughtful gentleman called Hanbury Tracy offered to take Geof, Derek's brother, and myself to Carthage to see whether we could find Derek's grave. To no avail - there were hastily dug graves everywhere. Such sadness - and waste!

A granddaughter was killed by a knife-wielding drug addict, who broke into the flat in which she was living. Young and very beautiful Lucy was horribly murdered. She was clever and artistic - such brutal stupidity I find hard to understand. More sorrow! But I digress. Back to the family. As I have already said my wife Joan and I operated to produce 7 children. For those mildly interested they are catalogued thus:

Boys: Martin - a vet married to a vet - 5 boys

Fergus - an electronic engineer - 2 boys

Duncan - brain damaged but very strong and useful

Girls: Ann - an out of the convent nun into social services and diet

Julie - painter and busy exhibiting. Married to Jason Potter from Harrow.

Faith - teaches at Somerset College of Art & Technology, Taunton - 2 boys and a lovely Sophie

Sheila - married to a mathematician at Cheltenham - 2 boys and 1 girl. Sheila also paints - mainly portraits.

A useful lot so on the whole a satisfactory effort on our part! A swathe of grandchildren whose birthdays come round all too often and are remembered with uncanny accuracy every year (Me? Ah fergittit!) by Joan.

# A tribute to my dear friend Joan

She's my wife actually. In our beginnings we had very little but she was good with money.

I told my friends that I always made the big decisions like "Should we keep the Atom Bomb" - she the minor ones about where to send the children to school.

The arrangement was beneficial especially for the children.

Joan was well versed in mechanics having been an A.T.S. driver for several years, stationed in Scotland and having to transport POW's to their various destinations and having to cope with the maintenance of the vehicles she was driving.

She became driver to Royalty and for several months was driver to General Frieberg the Commander of the New Zealand and Maori forces.

On many occasions Joan had to find destinations considerable distances away by having a map on her lap: there were no road signs in those days.

During the war I came across A.T.S. drivers who always looked smart and had presence and remembered thinking I wouldn't mind possessing one of those eventually!

Well done Joan - she remembers all the birthdays of children and grandchildren. And she's an excellent cook and in her element when preparing a meal for a crowd of relatives.